Bond

Non-verbal Reasoning
10 Minute Tests

8–9 years

Alison Primrose

OXFORD
UNIVERSITY PRESS

Which is the odd one out?

Example

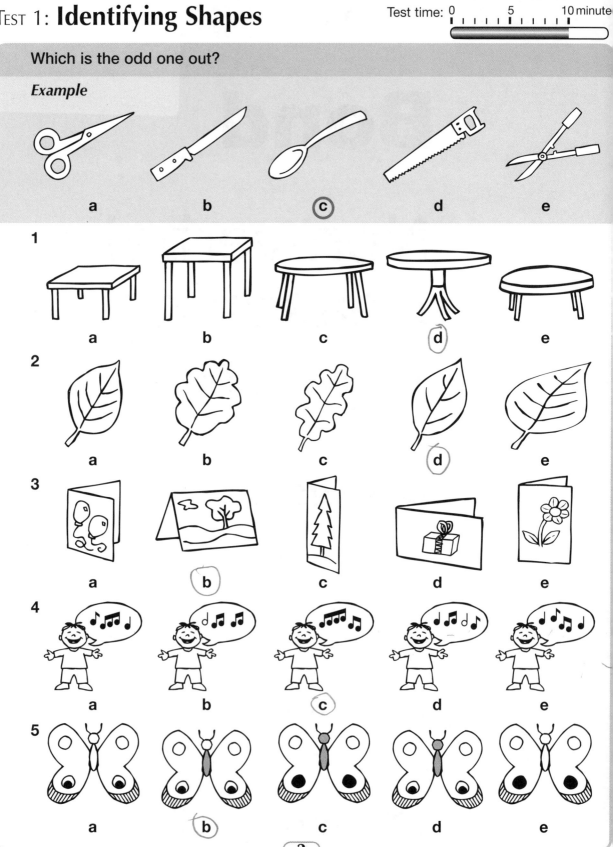

1

2

3

4

5

Which picture or pattern completes the second pair in the same way as the first pair?

Example

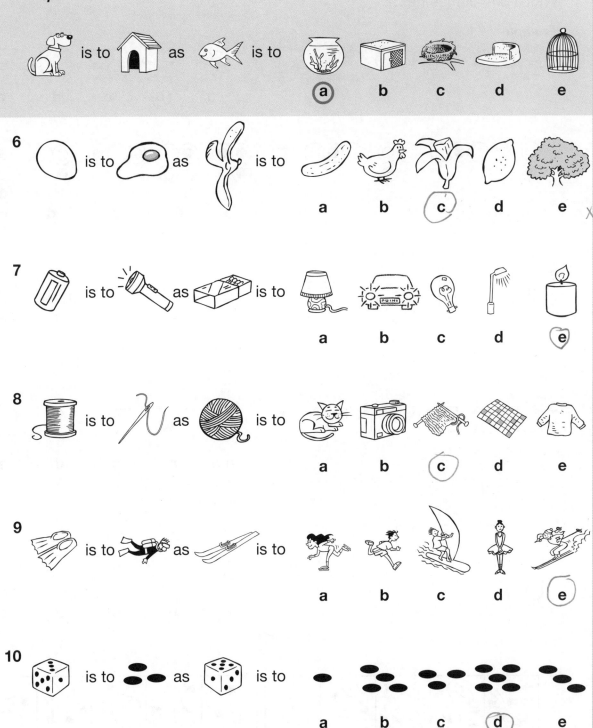

6 is to as is to

a   b   c   d   e

7 is to as is to

a   b   c   d   e

8 is to as is to

a   b   c   d   e

9 is to as is to

a   b   c   d   e

10 is to as is to

a   b   c   d   e

3

Total

Test time: 0   5   10 minutes

Which one comes next?

Example

a   (b)   c   d   e

1

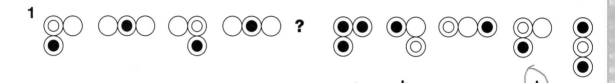

a   b   c   (d)   e

2

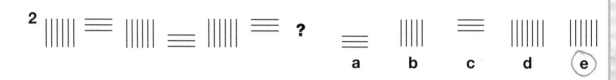

a   b   c   d   (e)

3

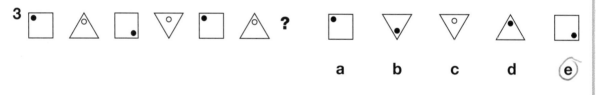

a   b   c   d   (e)

4

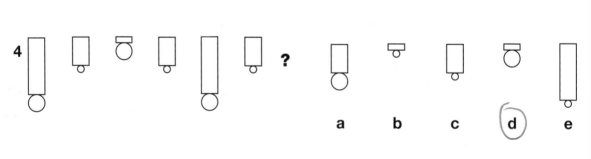

a   b   c   (d)   e

5

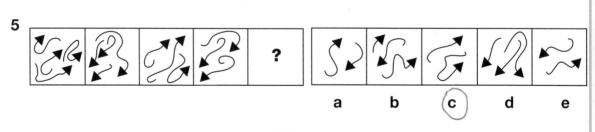

a   b   (c)   d   e

Which shape or picture completes the larger grid?

Example

a   b   ⓒ   d   e

6

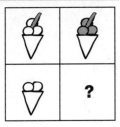

a   b   c   ⓓ   e

7

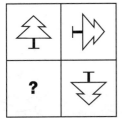

a   ⓑ   c   d   e

8

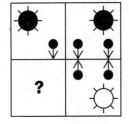

a   b   c   ⓓ   e

9

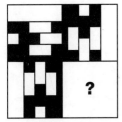

a   ⓑ   c   ⓓ   e

10

   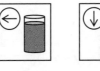

ⓐ   b   c   d   e

Total

Which is the odd one out?

Example

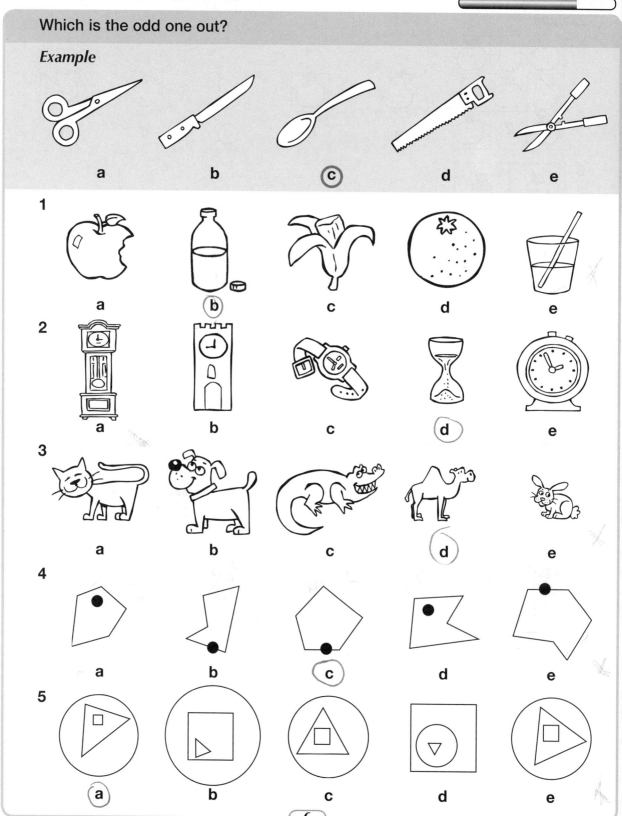

Which picture or pattern completes the second pair in the same way as the first pair?

Example

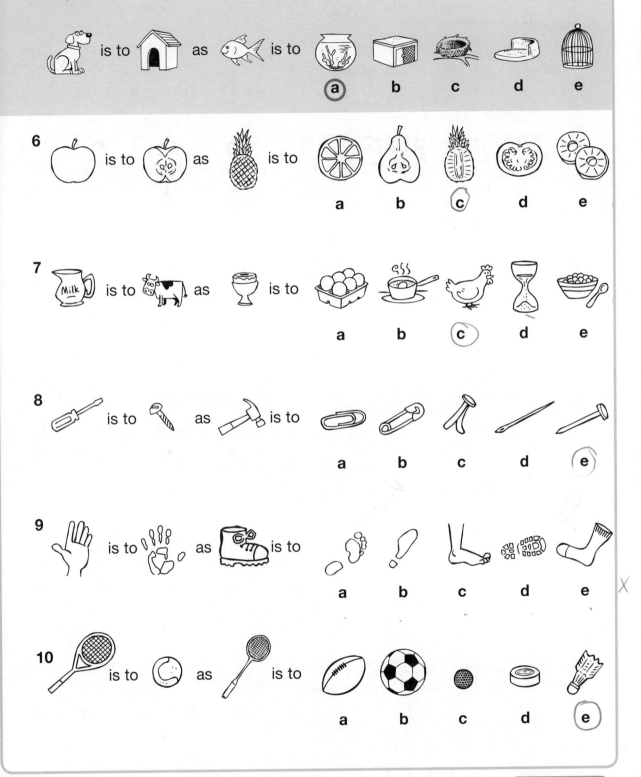

Total

TEST 4: **Missing Shapes**

 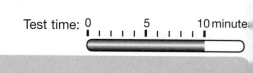

Which one comes next?

Example

1
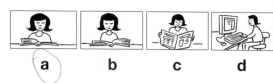

2

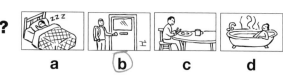

3

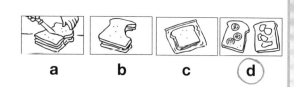

4

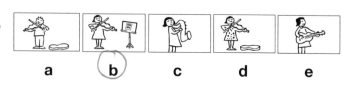

5
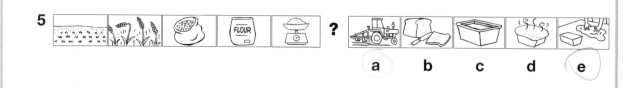

Which shape or pattern comes next?

6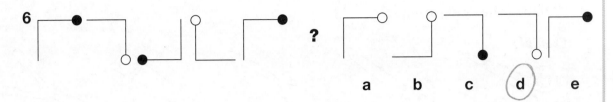

                                                         a   b   c   **d**   e

7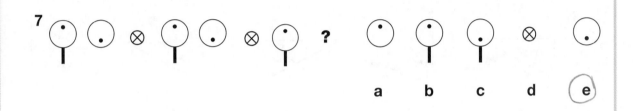

                       a   b   c   d   **e**

8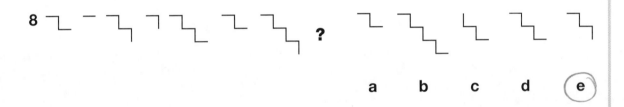

                       a   b   c   d   **e**

9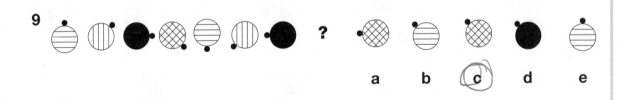

                       a   b   **c**   d   e

10

                       a   b   c   d   e

Time for a break! Go to Puzzle Page 38 ▶

Total

Which is the odd one out?

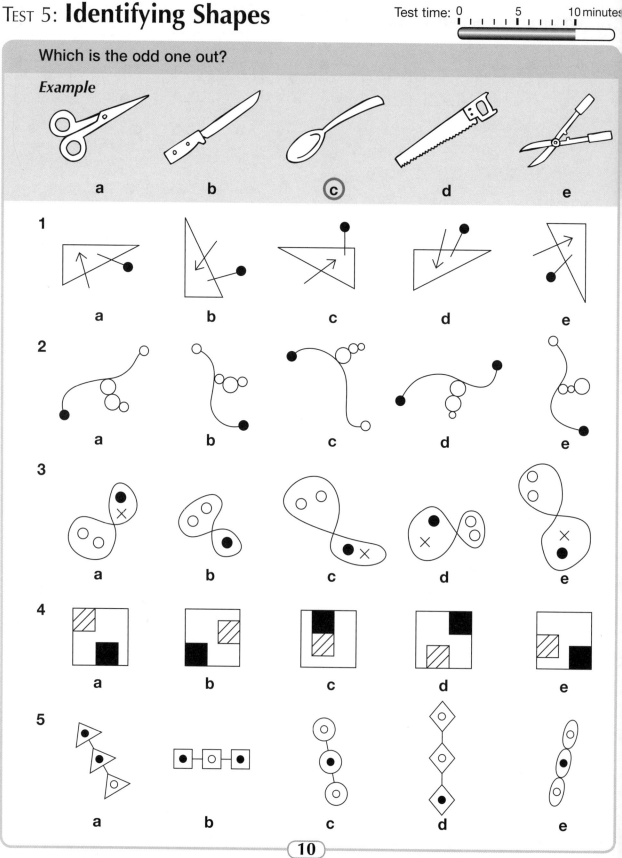

Example

a   b   ⓒ   d   e

1

a   b   c   d   e

2

a   b   c   d   e

3

a   b   c   d   e

4

a   b   c   d   e

5

a   b   c   d   e

Which picture or pattern completes the second pair in the same way as the first pair?

Example

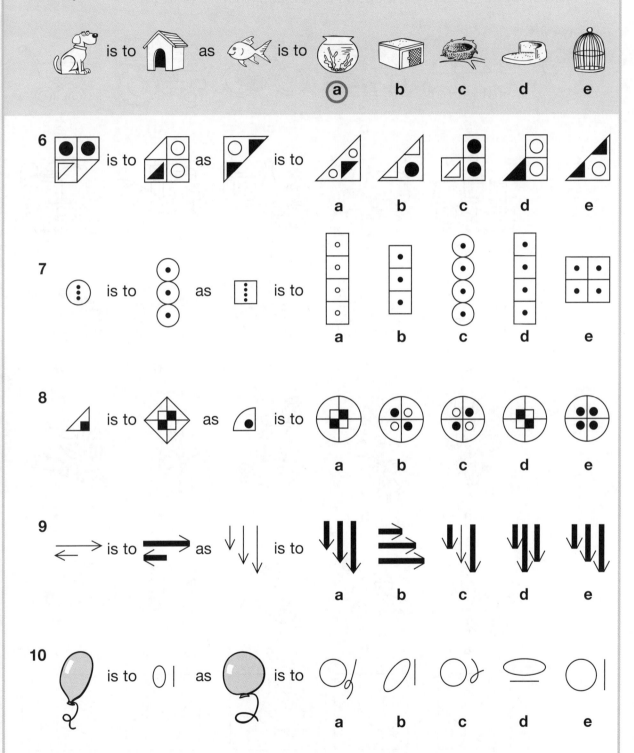

Total

Test time: 0 .... 5 .... 10 minutes

In which larger picture or shape is the smaller picture hidden?

Example

a   b   c   (d)   e

1

a   b   c   d   e

2

a   b   c   d   e

3

a   b   c   d   e

4

a   b   c   d   e

5

a   b   c   d   e

12

Which shape or picture completes the larger grid?

Example

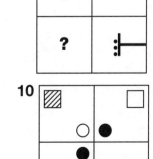

a   b   ⓒ   d   e

6

a   b   c   d   e

7

a   b   c   d   e

8

a   b   c   d   e

9

a   b   c   d   e

10

a   b   c   d   e

Total

Which is the odd one out?

Example

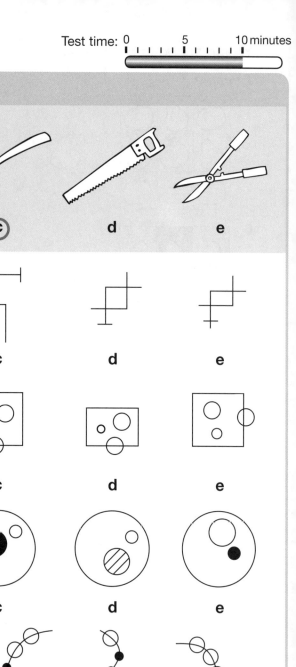

   a   b   ⓒ   d   e

1

   a   b   c   d   e

2

   a   b   c   d   e

3

   a   b   c   d   e

4

   a   b   c   d   e

5

   a   b   c   d   e

Which picture or pattern completes the second pair in the same way as the first pair?

Example

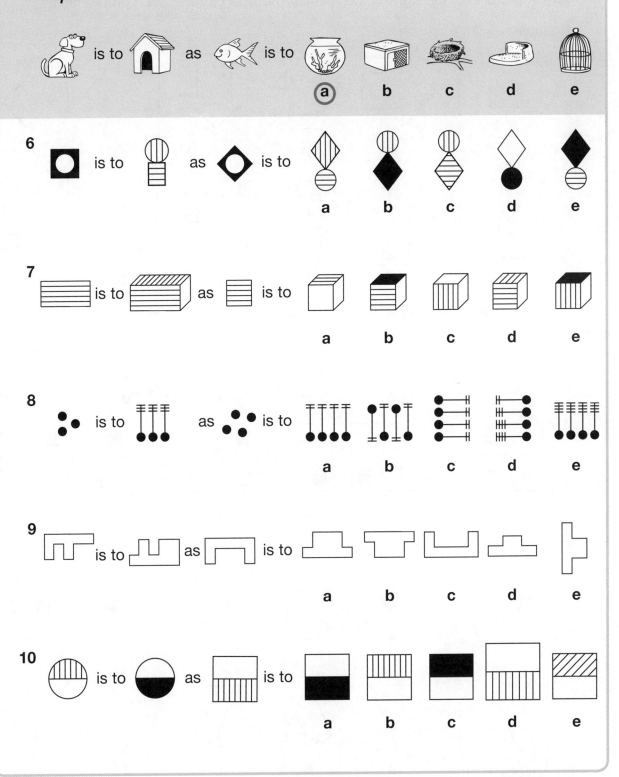

Total

Which picture on the right is the reflection of the picture given on the left?

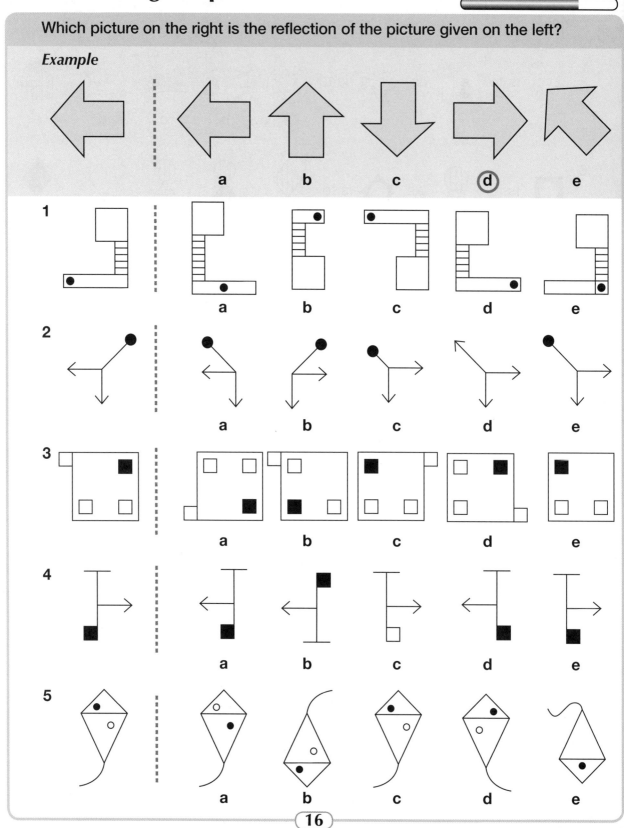

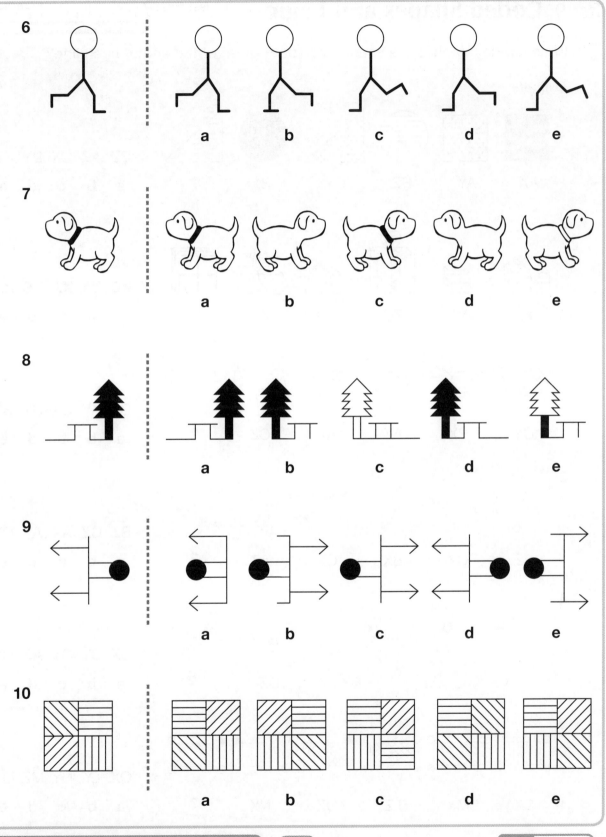

Which code matches the shape or pattern given at the end of each line?

Example

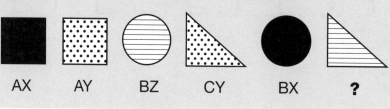

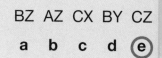

AX	AY	BZ	CY	BX	?

BZ AZ CX BY CZ
a   b   c   d   (e)

1

  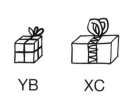

XB   YA   ZC   YB   XC   ?

ZB YA XA XC ZA
a   b   c   d   e

2

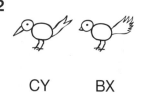 

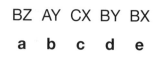

CY   BX   AZ   AX   CZ   ?

BZ AY CX BY BX
a   b   c   d   e

3

  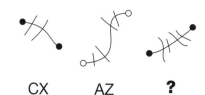

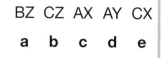

AZ   CY   BX   CX   AZ   ?

BZ CZ AX AY CX
a   b   c   d   e

4

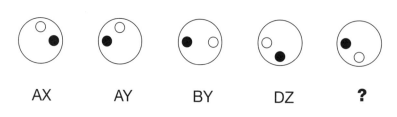

AX   AY   BY   DZ   ?

BX DY CY AZ CX
a   b   c   d   e

5

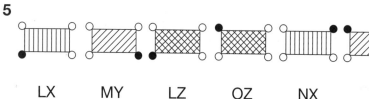

LX   MY   LZ   OZ   NX   ?

OX LY NY MZ OY
a   b   c   d   e

18

6

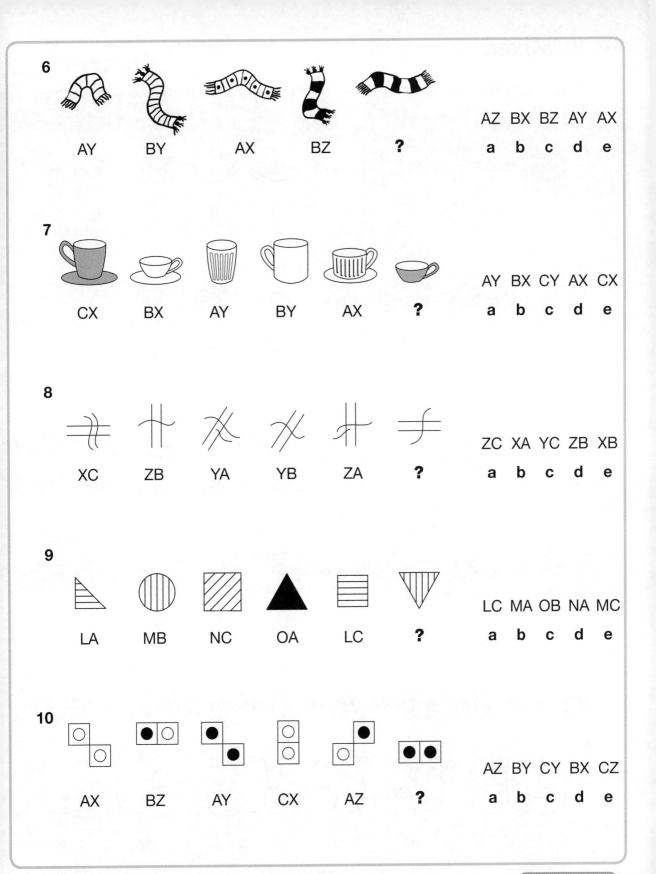

AY   BY   AX   BZ   ?

AZ BX BZ AY AX
a   **b**   **c**   **d**   **e**

7

CX   BX   AY   BY   AX   ?

AY BX CY AX CX
a   **b**   **c**   **d**   **e**

8

XC   ZB   YA   YB   ZA   ?

ZC XA YC ZB XB
a   **b**   **c**   **d**   **e**

9

LA   MB   NC   OA   LC   ?

LC MA OB NA MC
a   **b**   **c**   **d**   **e**

10

AX   BZ   AY   CX   AZ   ?

AZ BY CY BX CZ
a   **b**   **c**   **d**   **e**

Total

Which picture or pattern completes the second pair in the same way as the first pair?

1

                                                       a   b   c   d   e

2

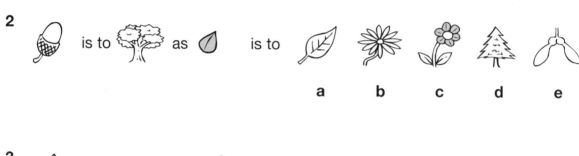

                                                       a   b   c   d   e

3

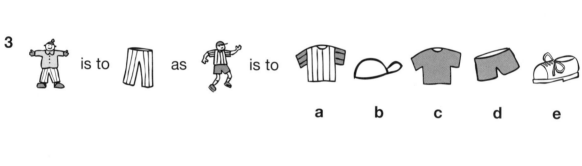

                                                       a   b   c   d   e

4

                                                       a   b   c   d   e

Which picture on the right is the reflection of the picture given on the left?

5

                                a   b   c   d   e

6

a   b   c   d   e

Which code matches the shape or pattern given at the end of each line?

7

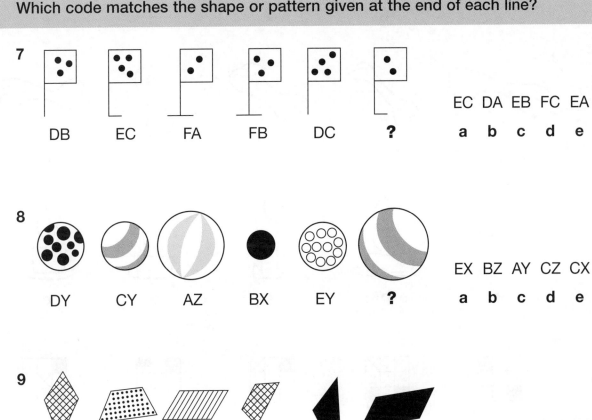

DB   EC   FA   FB   DC   **?**

EC DA EB FC EA
a   b   c   d   e

8

DY   CY   AZ   BX   EY   **?**

EX BZ AY CZ CX
a   b   c   d   e

9

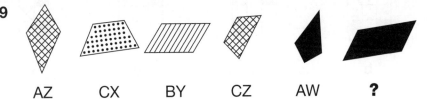

AZ   CX   BY   CZ   AW   **?**

AX BZ BW CW AY
a   b   c   d   e

10

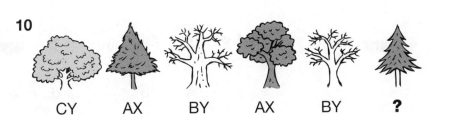

CY   AX   BY   AX   BY   **?**

AX CY BX CX AY
a   b   c   d   e

Total

Which is the odd one out?

1
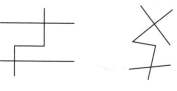   

a   b   c   d   e

2

a   b   c   d   e

3

a   b   c   d   e

4

a   b   c   d   e

Which one comes next?

5
      ?

a   b   c   d   e

Answers

TEST 1: Identifying Shapes

1 d
2 d
3 b
4 c
5 b
6 a
7 e
8 c
9 e
10 d

TEST 2: Missing Shapes

1 d
2 e
3 e
4 d
5 c
6 d
7 b
8 d
9 d
10 a

TEST 3: Identifying Shapes

1 d
2 d
3 c
4 e
5 d
6 c
7 c
8 e
9 d
10 e

TEST 4: Missing Shapes

1 a
2 b
3 d
4 b
5 e
6 d
7 e
8 e
9 c
10 d

TEST 5: Identifying Shapes

1 c
2 d
3 b
4 c
5 e
6 b
7 d
8 c
9 e
10 e

TEST 6: Missing Shapes

1 d
2 c
3 e
4 b
5 c
6 d
7 d
8 e
9 c
10 d

TEST 7: Identifying Shapes

1 e
2 d
3 b
4 c
5 c
6 c
7 d
8 e
9 a
10 c

TEST 8: Rotating Shapes

1 d
2 e
3 c
4 d
5 d
6 d
7 c
8 d
9 c
10 e

TEST 9: Coded Shapes and Logic

1 e
2 d
3 c
4 c
5 e
6 a
7 c
8 e
9 b
10 b

Answers

TEST 10: **Mixed**	TEST 13: **Mixed**	TEST 16: **Mixed**
1 d	**1** d	**1** e
2 c	**2** e	**2** b
3 d	**3** a	**3** d
4 e	**4** c	**4** b
5 c	**5** d	**5** d
6 b	**6** e	**6** e
7 e	**7** d	**7** d
8 d	**8** d	**8** e
9 c	**9** e	**9** c
10 e	**10** b	**10** c

TEST 11: **Mixed**	TEST 14: **Mixed**	TEST 17: **Mixed**
1 e	**1** d	**1** c
2 d	**2** e	**2** c
3 b	**3** b	**3** e
4 e	**4** c	**4** d
5 c	**5** d	**5** e
6 d	**6** a	**6** d
7 d	**7** b	**7** e
8 d	**8** e	**8** c
9 d	**9** c	**9** e
10 e	**10** d	**10** b

TEST 12: **Mixed**	TEST 15: **Mixed**	TEST 18: **Mixed**
1 e	**1** c	**1** e
2 b	**2** d	**2** c
3 c	**3** c	**3** d
4 e	**4** a	**4** e
5 d	**5** c	**5** d
6 c	**6** d	**6** e
7 d	**7** d	**7** c
8 c	**8** d	**8** e
9 a	**9** e	**9** d
10 c	**10** c	**10** e

Answers

Puzzle ❶

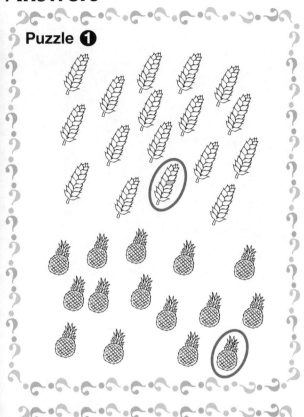

Puzzle ❸

A 8
B 1
C 6
D 3
E 4
F 2
G 7
H 5

Puzzle ❷

Puzzle ❹

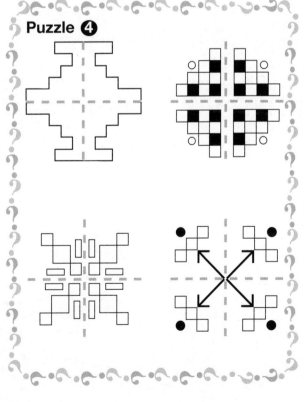

Answers

Puzzle ❺

6

                                           a   b   c   d   e

7  ?

                                        a   b   c   d   e

Which picture on the right is the reflection of the picture given on the left?

8

       a   b   c   d   e

9

       a   b   c   d   e

10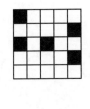

       a   b   c   d   e

Total

Which picture or pattern completes the second pair in the same way as the first pair?

1

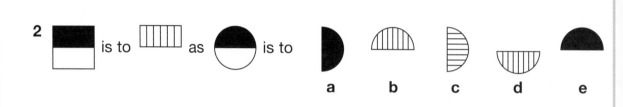

a b c d e

2

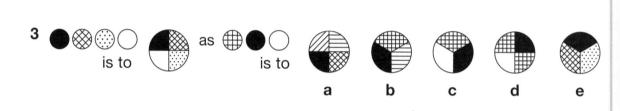

a b c d e

3

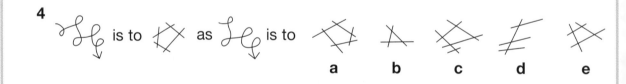

a b c d e

4

is to   as   is to

a b c d e

Which one comes next?

5

?

a b c d e

6  **?**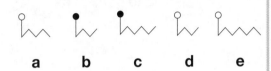

a   b   c   d   e

7 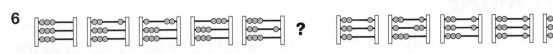 **?**

a   b   c   d   e

In which larger shape is the smaller shape hidden?

8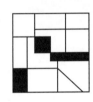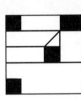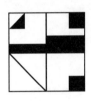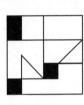

a   b   c   d   e

9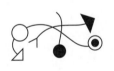

a   b   c   d   e

10

a   b   c   d   e

Test time: 0   5   10 minutes

Which picture or pattern completes the second pair in the same way as the first pair?

1

is to ... as ... is to

            a   b   c   d   e

2

is to ... as ... is to

            a   b   c   d   e

3

is to ... as ... is to

            a   b   c   d   e

Which one comes next?

4

... ?

            a   b   c   d   e

5

... ?

            a   b   c   d   e

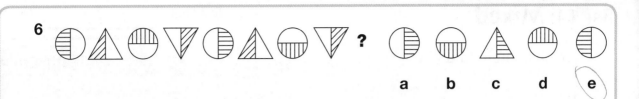

6
a   b   c   d   e

7
a   b   c   d   e

Which code matches the shape or pattern given at the end of each line?

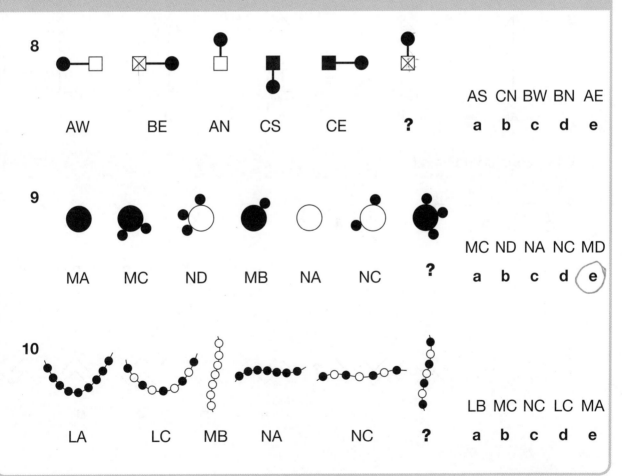

8

AW   BE   AN   CS   CE   **?**

AS CN BW BN AE
a   b   c   d   e

9

MA   MC   ND   MB   NA   NC   **?**

MC ND NA NC MD
a   b   c   d   e

10

LA   LC   MB   NA   NC   **?**

LB MC NC LC MA
a   b   c   d   e

Total

Test time: 0 | | | | | 5 | | | | | 10 minutes

Which is the odd one out?

1

   a   b   c   d   e

2

   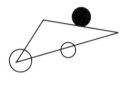

   a   b   c   d   e

3

   a   b   c   d   e

Which one comes next?

4

   **?**

                       a   b   c   d   e

5

 **?**

                     a   b   c   d   e

6 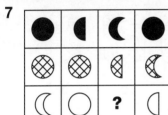 **?**

a   b   c   d   e

Which shape or picture completes the larger grid?

7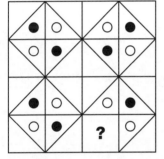

a   b   c   d   e

8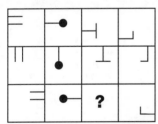

a   b   c   d   e

9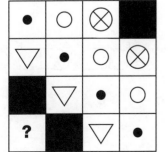

a   b   c   d   e

10

Total

Test time: 0 — 5 — 10 minutes

Which picture or pattern completes the second pair in the same way as the first pair?

1 is to as is to

      a   b   c   d   e

2  is to as is to

      a   b   c   d   e

3 is to as is to

      a   b   c   d   e

Which one comes next?

4  **?**

      a   b   c   d   e

5   **?**

      a   b   c   d   e

In which larger shape is the smaller shape hidden?

6   a   b   c   d   e

7   a   b   c   d   e

Which picture on the right is the reflection of the picture given on the left?

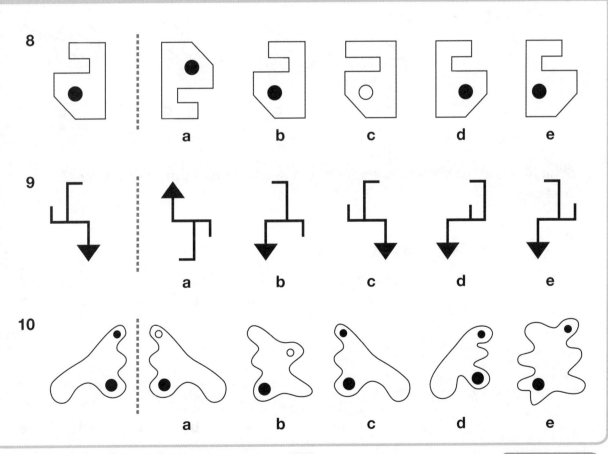

8   a   b   c   d   e

9   a   b   c   d   e

10   a   b   c   d   e

Total

Test time: 0 | | | | | | 5 | | | | | 10 minutes

Which is the odd one out?

1

     a   b   c   d   e

2

     a   b   c   d   e

3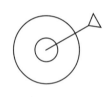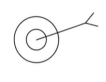

     a   b   c   d   e

Which picture or pattern completes the second pair in the same way as the first pair?

4 is to as is to

                                             a   b   c   d   e

5  is to as is to

                                             a   b   c   d   e

6 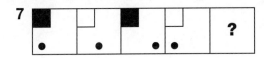 is to as is to

a   b   c   d   e

Which one comes next?

7 ?

a   b   c   d   e

8 🖊▲🦪▽🖊▲🦪 ?

,   △   ▼   🦪   ▽

a   b   c   d   e

Which picture on the right is the reflection of the picture given on the left?

9 ┊

        a   b   c   d   e

10 ┊

        a   b   c   d   e

Time for a break! Go to Puzzle Page 41 ▶   **33**   Total ▢

Which picture or pattern completes the second pair in the same way as the first pair?

1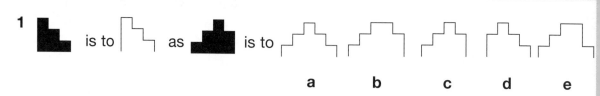

                a   b   c   d   e

2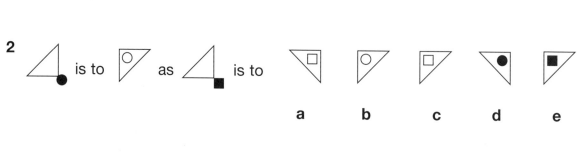

                a   b   c   d   e

3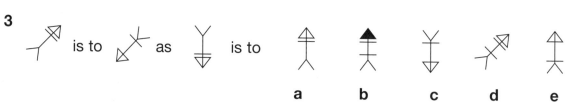

                a   b   c   d   e

Which one comes next?

4 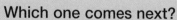 **?**

                a   b   c   d   e

5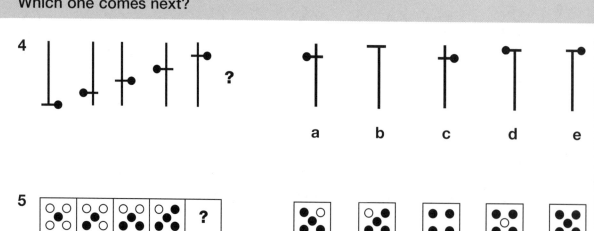

                a   b   c   d   e

6  **?**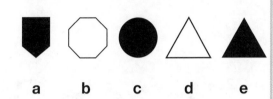

                                                   a   b   c   d   e

7 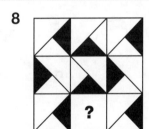   **?**

                                                   a   b   c   d   e

Which shape or picture completes the larger grid?

8 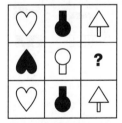

                               a   b   c   d   e

9

                               a   b   c   d   e

10 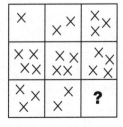

                               a   b   c   d   e

Total

Test time: 0 |||||| 5 ||||||| 10 minutes

Which one comes next?

1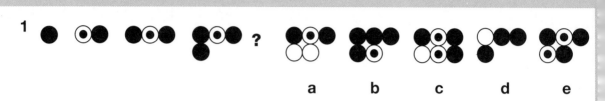

           a   b   c   d   e

2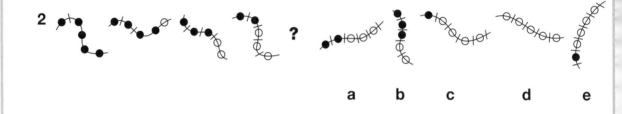

           a   b   c   d   e

3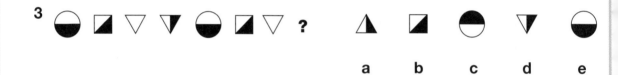

           a   b   c   d   e

4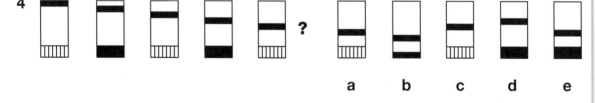

           a   b   c   d   e

Which shape or picture completes the larger grid?

5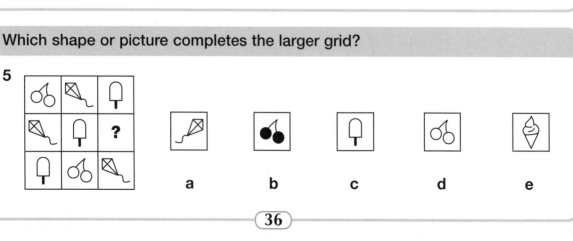

           a   b   c   d   e

6

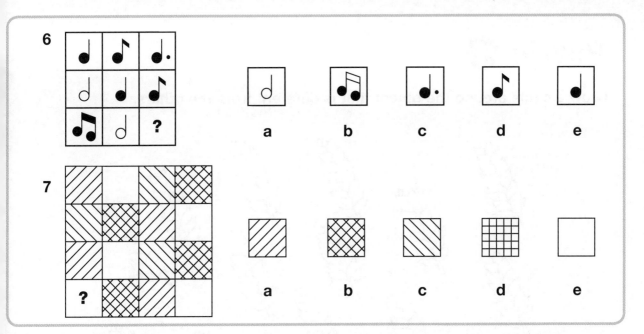

7

Which code matches the shape or pattern given at the end of each line?

8

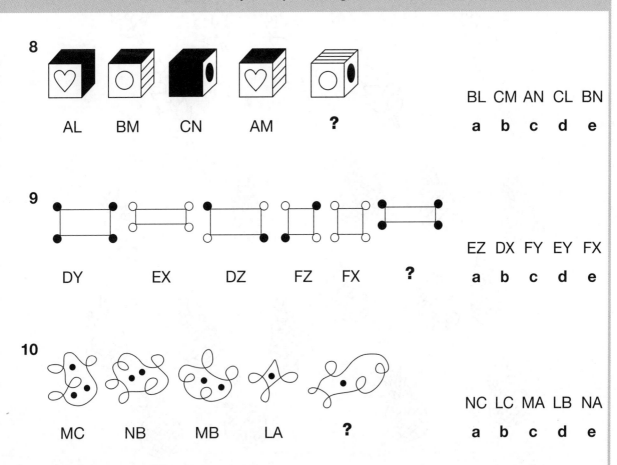

AL   BM   CN   AM   ?

BL CM AN CL BN
a   b   c   d   e

9

DY   EX   DZ   FZ   FX   ?

EZ DX FY EY FX
a   b   c   d   e

10

MC   NB   MB   LA   ?

NC LC MA LB NA
a   b   c   d   e

Puzzle ①

Draw a circle around the object that is different from the others.

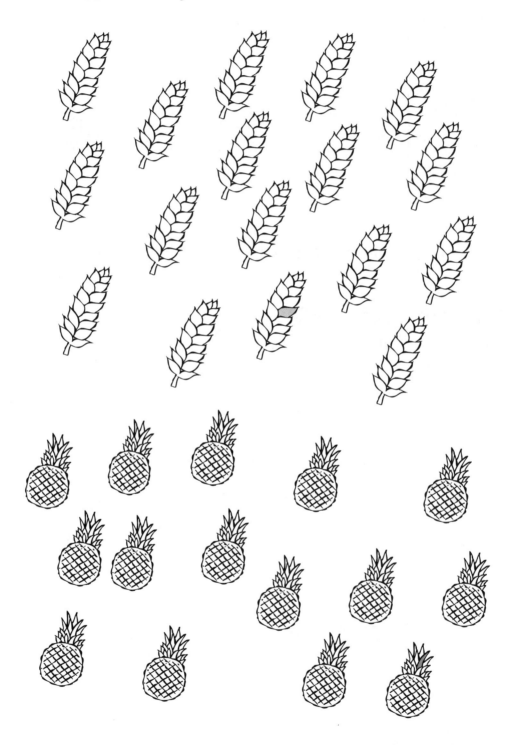

Puzzle ❷

Match the pattern to the shadow of its mirror image.

Puzzle ③

Match the missing squares to the letters given below.

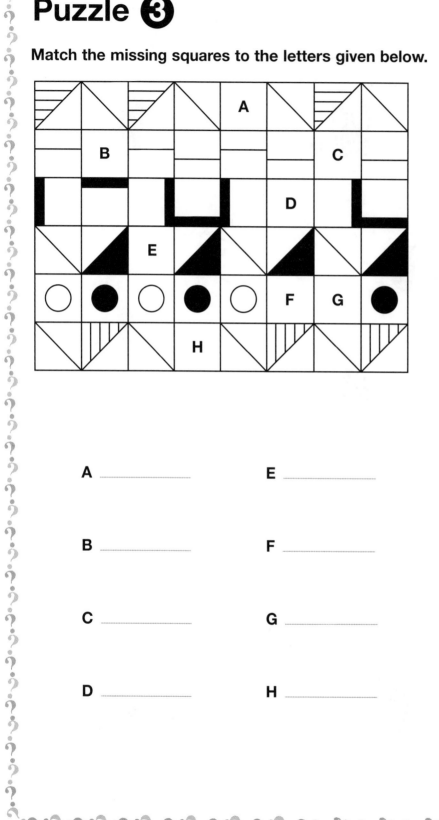

1

2

3

4

5

6

7

8

A ....

E ....

B ....

F ....

C ....

G ....

D ....

H ....

Puzzle 4️⃣

Complete these patterns.

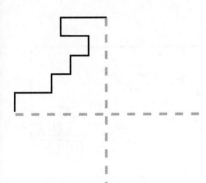

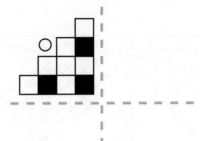

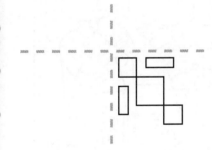

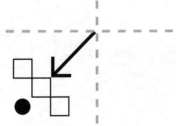

Puzzle ⑤

Where is this shape hidden in the picture?

Progress Grid

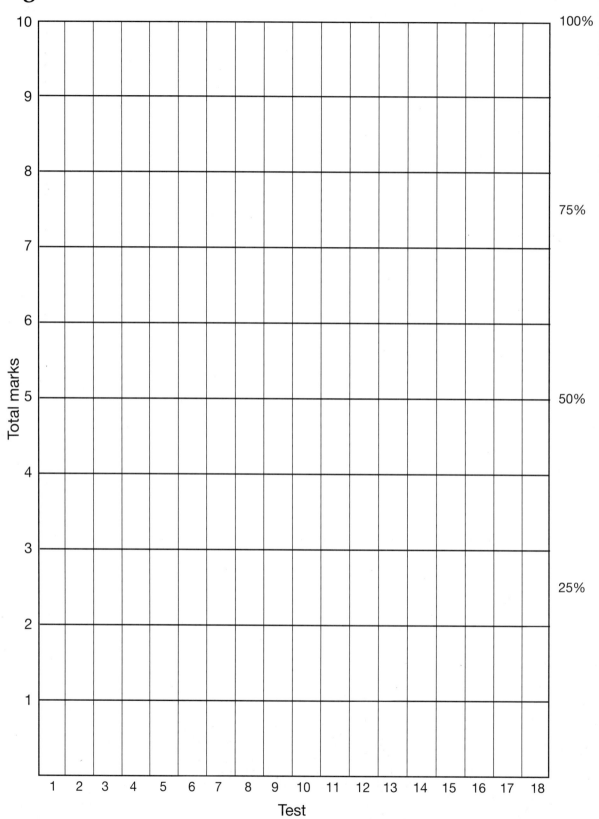